NAVAJO WOMEN: *Sáanii*

NAVAJO WOMEN: *Sáanii*

BETTY REID

PHOTOGRAPHY AND FOREWORD BY

KENJI KAWANO

RIO NUEVO PUBLISHERS

TUCSON, ARIZONA

Rio Nuevo Publishers®
P.O. Box 5250, Tucson, Arizona 85703-0250
(520) 623-9558, www.rionuevo.com

Library of Congress Cataloging-in-Publication Data

Reid, Betty.
Navajo women : Sáanii / by Betty Reid ; photography by Kenji Kawano.
p. cm.
ISBN 978-1-933855-05-9
1. Navajo women—Biography. 2. Navajo women—Social conditions. I. Title.
E99.N3R43 2007
305.89'972—dc22
2007015370

Design: Karen Schober, Seattle, Washington.

Printed in Korea.

10 9 8 7 6 5 4 3 2 1

This book is dedicated to my extended Navajo family, shepherds on the northeastern rim of the Grand Canyon. They had to be physically stronger than the dark granite rock in order to survive the dust storms, snowstorms, hail, and intense heat. They were of an earth-based faith. They made journeys, clutching their bags filled with corn pollen, to Bidáá–The Edge–and sprinkled the yellow dust into the deep chasm of the rim that falls off into a haze of multitiered shadows. They prayed to the Colorado River, which they knew as a holy deity with a long soul.

American history books are written about how the Southwest was settled by pioneers. I believe my elders were the pioneers who settled the rugged and sprawling edge of western Navajo Nation.

This book is dedicated to the children, in-laws, and grandchildren of Edith, my paternal grandmother. Without these relatives, I would not have stories to share.

—BETTY REID

Dedicated to the Navajo women who believe in a better tomorrow for their Nation and its people. This book grew out of many years of photographing Navajo women who live on the reservation, within the four sacred mountains.

—KENJI KAWANO

CONTENTS

FOREWORD

When I meet old Navajo women, I say, "Yá'át'ééh shimá," or "Hello my mother."

NAVAJOS SAY, "THE EARTH IS OUR MOTHER and the sun is our father." It is a beautiful way to view the world. I came to this "Mother Earth" on the Navajo Indian Reservation in March 1974. Five months earlier, in November of 1973, I had left Tokyo, Japan, to go to Los Angeles, California, to photograph America. I wanted to complete a portfolio to take back to Tokyo and to exhibit the photographs of America. But I could not find the subject I wanted to photograph in L.A.

One person told me about a Navajo Indian who lived on a reservation. The Navajo Reservation is located in Arizona, New Mexico, and Utah. I was excited about photographing today's American Indian as my project. When I was growing up I saw many Western movies and was always sympathetic toward the American Indians. I felt that I had to go to Indian Country. I did not know the Navajos or their reservation, but I decided to go photograph Navajos.

I needed a place to stay on the reservation, and I managed to live with a Navajo family in Fort Defiance, Arizona. Walking around, I could not believe my eyes that Navajo people looked like Japanese. I began to photograph the Navajo people, but since I did not speak English or Navajo, it was difficult to communicate.

After four months in Fort Defiance I moved to Ganado, Arizona, where I worked as a gas station attendant to support myself. I photographed Ganado and its people. Being in Ganado was an adventure every day, and I had many new experiences that I never had in Japan.

I learned more and more about Navajo customs and traditions, which helped me to understand Navajo people and their life. I found out that Navajo women were unlike women of Japan. They were strong and made decisions in the household. Navajo women are persevering and have big hearts. Also, they are patient in the environment of everyday life.

In the Navajo tradition, when a young couple marries the bridegroom moves to the bride's home to support her family. In Japan the opposite happens. I married my Navajo wife back in 1978. Since then I've learned more about Navajo customs and Navajo language from her. I began to understand the Navajo world. When I meet old Navajo women I say, "*Yá'át'ééh shimá*," or "Hello my mother," then shake their hands. Or I might say to someone younger, "*shidezhi*," or "my younger sister."

Another experience I had was with my mother-in-law. Back in the 1980s, on Mother's Day with my in-laws, she was kneeling down to the dry earth outside her home, and she said a prayer looking down at the ground. She poured water on the ground and said, "Happy Mother's Day." I had never thought of that gratitude to the earth on Mother's Day.

Today's Navajo women are not just wives. We have many professional women as well as many who keep the Navajo traditional ways. We need both the professional and the traditional women to make progress and to preserve Navajo traditions.

I've met so many Navajo people and visited them all over the reservation, and I have many good memories of people and places.

I would like to say thank you to all the Navajo women who understood my calling to photograph them. Without their understanding I could not publish the photographs.

To the book's editor, Carrie Stusse, thank you for your help and patience.

To my wife, Ruth, who always encourages and supports me and my photography, thank you.

Ahéhee' to all.

KENJI KAWANO

WINDOW ROCK, NAVAJO NATION, ARIZONA

INTRODUCTION

We Diné (the people) are the children of Asdzáá Nádleehí, Changing Woman. She is a holy deity found on Gobernador Knob in New Mexico. She quickly grew up, and a Blessing Way—a sacred ritual that sets one on a positive life journey—was performed at her kinaalda. *This is a ritual still practiced today at a girl's first and second menses. Changing Woman's chief role was to procreate. She gave birth to twin boys, Child Born for the Water (Tó Bájíshhini) and Monster Slayer (Naayéé Neizghání), who killed Ye'ii Tsoh, large monsters that roamed and terrorized people in the lower world. The boys traveled to their father, the Sun (Yádilhil Shitaa' Jíhonaa'éí), for intelligence and weapons to slay the giants.*

Changing Woman traveled from her birthplace to the western edge of the Nation and resides there. Today she's the spiritual deity medicine people identify first when they start prayers. Asdzáá Nádleehí biyázhí nishlí...I am the child of Changing Woman. That's what I was told by my elders.

—JEANETTE REED,
a retired sheepherder who lives in Tuba City. The eighty-two-year-old elder is of the Tó dích'ii'nii (Bitter Water Clan), and is born for Kin yaa'áanii (Towering House People).

THIS BOOK IS A SNAPSHOT OF WOMEN living the *iiná*, or life, arranged in a lifecycle like the interior of a classic round Navajo house called a hogan. Planted into the earth-shaped life are four cardinal directions, each representing a stage of life with certain expectations. The east is birth and represents the white swath of light seen at dawn and signifies thinking. The sky-blue south symbolizes water and is a stage for planning among teenagers and young adults. The west is yellow for corn pollen, or the color of *tádídíín*, which is used to communicate with the Holy People, as an offering or to cleanse in a ritual, and is the phase for adults, who apply their knowledge to life. Maturity and the elderly are tied to the north (black) direction, where a Navajo person is built up in wisdom and strength.

Traditional Diné (Navajo) elders say we live in the Fifth World. This is a world that sparkles with everything magical. It is the pinnacle of four previous journeys, each bringing the People to a higher level of life. The elders tell of a journey from the belly inside the earth. The People fled flood and chaos.

Eventually, after many thousands of years, the Diné ancestors settled into what is now known as northeastern Arizona. The 27,000 square miles of the Navajo Nation lie in parts of northeastern Arizona, northwestern New Mexico, and southern Utah. It is said the Nation is the size of West Virginia. The Nation was not as large in 1868 when Navajos were freed from Fort Sumner, New Mexico, where they completed the Long Walk and were held captive for four years. General James Carleton and a scout named Christopher "Kit" Carson rounded up Navajos and sent them to Fort Sumner as punishment for raiding settlements in New Mexico and other tribal villages. Historians recorded the Navajo population at 16,000 in 1868 when they returned to their country.

There, over many generations, the people moved from a hunting-and-raiding culture into a simple pastoral way of life, herding sheep and goats amid the red sand cliffs, grama grass, and sagebrush of the high desert plateaus. The land of the Diné is surrounded by four sacred mountains—Blanca Peak, Mount Taylor, the San Francisco Peaks, and Mount Hesperus. Some Navajos look at Navajo lands as a hogan, bound by the four sacred mountains. Gobernador Knob and Heurfano Mesa are situated to the east as though they are the entrance into Navajo Country—the doorway into the hogan-shaped country. Some Navajos believe Gobernador Knob is the heart of Navajo Country, while Huerfano Mesa represents its lungs.

Some Navajo women hold onto the shepherd's lifestyle. But many others have blended easily into the fabric of American society. Nine-to-five jobs fuel their cravings for iPods, computers, designer clothes, fast cars, education, and modern entertainment—even Gucci or Coach bags. Like other American women, some have fallen victim to the darker side of alcohol and drug abuse.

In the glittery Fifth World, faiths and philosophy changed. Diné women adapted. The Navajo language and philosophy have suffered neglect as women sought out a modern Western education. Many moved out of the protective circle of the four sacred mountains surrounding Navajo Country. But whether they live on the land or in big cities, Navajo women continue to be the cornerstone of a matriarchal and matrilineal society that defines identity through a mother's bloodline. Children, for example, are given their mother's clans. Property is passed down from mother to daughter. Once relegated to caring for the home front, many Navajo women have used modern education to achieve careers. There are more Navajo women than men, for example, leaving community colleges with associate degrees and universities with bachelor degrees.

"I think that as a matrilineal society where our primary identities are rooted in our maternal clans, we tend to be harder on our daughters than we are on our sons, and have great expectations of them," says Dr. Jennifer Nez Denetdale, a history professor at the University of New Mexico in Albuquerque. "I think in many ways we still draw on those images of powerful female deities like Changing Woman."

The spiritual deities play a role in the lives of Navajo women in numerous ways. It could be a daily prayer that mentions Changing Woman, it could be during a kinaalda when Changing Woman's rite of passage is reenacted, or it could be a prayer for perseverance and strength. Pauline Whitesinger, an eighty-year-old elder, used the sacred powers of the mountains and women deities as a spiritual shield when Congress ordered her to move off land partitioned to the neighboring Hopi tribe. The feisty elder continues to live at Sweet Water Wide House on Hopi land. The government told her it would provide a large home for her if she moved away from the land from which she was born and raised. Whitesinger never considered it an option.

"If I [had] received an American education, I probably would have moved when the government dangled that house with running water and electricity in front of me," Whitesinger explained in Navajo. "That's not me. Why would I move out of the four sacred mountains and land where Changing Woman walked? Why run away from my songs that are intertwined with the land here? Why move away from my prayers? When I pray, I say, 'I want to be as strong as Mother Earth.' I don't say, 'I want to be as strong as that tall glass building.' I identify myself as a child of Changing Woman in my prayers. The land hears me here. How will it hear me when I move away?"

Whitesinger is a traditional Navajo woman. She sports a blue-and-white striped cotton shirt with red roses pinned at the neck with a safety pin. Her light-colored calico skirt flows with the wind. Her teal-colored socks accent her black sneakers. Whitesinger fails to see how traditional Navajo and American values align. She never attended school.

Carmen K. Begay, a science researcher who grew up in White Cone and now lives in Phoenix, Arizona, has packed a lot into four decades. Most recently, she joined the U.S. Navy to do her part in the war against terrorism. She is one of an estimated sixty Navajo women and 250 Navajo men currently serving in Iraq. Her rank is petty officer second class, a Navy yeoman. Begay holds a bachelor degree in microbiology and a master's degree in chemistry, both from Northern Arizona University, a college that looks upon the sacred peaks from the south. Begay also founded Only on the Rez, a miniature ornament business that sells tiny frybread or Navajo taco ornaments fashioned for holiday decorations. With the exception of some physical limitations and religious ceremonies, she believes the Navajo culture does not prohibit women from doing just about anything.

Genevieve Jackson, a former Navajo Nation councilwoman and manager of the Nation's Head Start program, is a champion of Navajo women. "It's not a mystery that our women achieve at high levels," Jackson notes. "I was raised by my parents, who told me there is no limit to how I shape and design my life. I could be a mother, I could be in the military, I could be a teacher, I could be a doctor, or I could be a leader of my people. I chose to lead."

Women continue to meet challenges posed in the Fifth World. While more Navajo women than men live on the Nation, are registered to vote, and have a presence in medicine, law, social work, education, and health, their numbers are limited in politics. There are nine women on the eighty-eight-member Navajo council. Some blame Navajo cultural beliefs that prohibit women from reaching this level of leadership. The crux of their beliefs is tied to a quarrel that occurred as the Diné were moving up through four underworlds and split the genders.

Jackson is one of a handful of women who have gone after the top job as president of the Navajo Nation. She believes demographics are changing on the Nation. Fathers are absent in many homes, and women are forced to redouble their efforts to care for the family. Education seems to offer a solution for women to make a positive impact on the Nation's high unemployment rate.

These are stories and photographic renderings of the lives of contemporary Navajo women, *sáanii.* Today's women lead varied lives, from the Nation's rural communities to America's cities. Their life stories are arranged in the Navajo lifecycle, using the four cardinal directions. These are portraits of Navajo women.

EAST

CHILDHOOD

Sis Naajiní – Blanca Peak

CRADLED IN THE ARMS OF HER MOTHER, Giavanti Bischoff nurses at a lively McDonald's restaurant in Window Rock, the capital of the Navajo Nation in northeastern Arizona. The fidgety ten-month-old infant seems soothed by the hissing of hot oil and three noisy sisters feasting on French fries and chicken nuggets. The child's older sisters are excited about hopping in the "bounce house" at the carnival during the annual Navajo Nation Fair. They'll be united with other girls their age, carrying iPods and cell phones and speaking only in English. Giavanti and her sisters are Táchii'nii women, belonging to the Red Running into Water Clan. Giavanti is born for Beeshbiichii (German Clan). Their mother, Felecita, is also a Táchii'nii and is born for Bit'aa'nii, or the Leaf Clan.

Giavanti is destined to grow up in a radically different world than did the generations of Navajo women before her. For example, the year little Giavanti first attended the Nation's fair, Lynda Lovejoy from Crownpoint, New Mexico, made her mark on tribal history and became the first female to edge out

nine Navajo men in the primary election. Lovejoy, though she ultimately lost the presidential race, received distinction because she bucked an eight-decade tradition that only men can hold the top office of America's largest Indian tribe.

The odds are against Giavanti's learning to speak her native tongue, because she will grow up hearing English only. Giavanti's mother, Felecita, speaks only English, a trend that accounts for one-third of the Navajo population. The little girl and her family are members of the Morning Star Ministry Church and crisscross the Nation in a van hearing about the Christian god, as opposed to the Navajo deities that reside on the land.

Giavanti's mother envisions her youngest child entering college in twenty years, somewhere in a big city or a Nation border town, after completing a Christian high school education. Life in a big city appears to be the destiny of most Navajo youth today. A high unemployment rate—nearly 50 percent—and a lack of opportunity on the Navajo Nation force members off the reservation. Giavanti's father, for example, died in an auto wreck on a Colorado highway during his commute to work. Felecita, a twenty-eight-year-old widow who lacks a high school diploma and has only waitressing skills, is tempted to load the kids in the van and relocate to a big city. The young mother knows what life off the reservation has to offer.

Felecita's mother, a homemaker educated at Many Farms Boarding School, operated by the U.S. Bureau of Indian Affairs, moved away from the reservation as a child and eventually married a truck driver. The family moved back to the Navajo Nation from Idaho to care for ailing parents. What should have been a celebrated return to their roots instead turned into an unraveling of the family, recalls Felecita, then thirteen and the oldest child in the family. The teenager had enjoyed life in Idaho, where hair dryers whirred to life at the push of a button, hot water gushed out of a faucet, waste swirled away in water, and a heater warmed the home. Then the family moved into a tiny, octagonal-shaped hogan with a cement floor, minus electricity and infrastructure. Felecita quickly learned about poverty. With the snap of a finger, everything changed. She recalls, "The hogan had a tiny wood-burning stove, and the elders from the local Mormon church hauled water for us in water barrels."

The lure of alcohol beckoned. Felecita started to drink in middle school. Later, she dropped out of Navajo Pine High School. Before she walked out of the classroom, she met Giavanti's father, half German and half Navajo, whom she married. But then tragedy struck, and her husband was killed in an accident. She joined the ranks of single parents on the Navajo Nation. One-fourth of all homes on the reservation are run by single parents.

For a split second, as she tells her story, the spirit of the young mother seems crushed. She dabs fresh

tears from her face with a napkin. Then fire returns to her eyes.

"I could have started to drink again to cope with my intense grief," says Felecita, who had taken to partying during middle school as a way to cope with change. "But I chose not to, because I refuse to raise my kids like that. That is not what my late husband and I talked about. We wanted a Christian home, and our kids would attend Christian schools. I plan to get my kids there."

What drives her? "My prayers and the Lord," Felecita says. She packs little Giavanti in a stroller, gathers up the family, and starts ambling toward the fairgrounds.

Brigadier Brown, fifteen, is growing up in the Navajo Nation border town of Gallup, New Mexico, a sprawling city on Interstate 40 made famous by John Ford Westerns of the 1940s and by Route 66, which serves as its business artery. Brigadier's father, a Navajo

comedian in Gallup, threw his family for a loop when he gave his young daughter an unusual name after a military field officer's rank. The teenager, a budding actress and entertainer, is not embarrassed by the name and has no fear of performing.

In the old days, Navajos gave children names they could use like codes for protection in battle. The names were pumped with force and strength, a throwback to when the two hero twins in the Navajo creation story slew the people-munching giants, and to the nineteenth-century Navajo wars with the Spaniards, the U.S. Cavalry, and neighboring tribes. When the tribe was exposed to government-sponsored Christian missionaries who were invited into schools and imposed their philosophy, many Navajo girls turned up with names that had not been used in previous centuries, such as Betty, Elizabeth, Mary, Annie, Jean, or Alice. Later, the Navajo crowd gave children names like Tiffany, Britney, Bianca, or Ashlee.

Brigadier says the name fits her, because she aspires to see her name on the silver screen one day and plans to stroll down that famous red carpet in Hollywood. Before taking that glamorous walk, she is learning the ropes by traveling and writing comedy acts with her father. They work with a talent agency called Emergence Productions, which promotes Native entertainers.

Brigadier is a student at Gallup High School and a member of the Church of Jesus Christ of Latter-day Saints. She listens to country music, shops at the mall, and enjoys visits with her grandmother. She is part of the Honágháahnii (One Who Walks Around You Clan) and is born for Deesch'ii'nii (Start of the Red Streak Clan).

Brigadier does not speak Navajo. She worries about the fading Navajo traditions. Her peers are resorting to alcohol and substance abuse. She is concerned about the death of a pure Diné race, because she sees many Navajo women in interracial marriages.

Her mother, a tribal worker, manages the father-and-daughter gigs on the Nation and in border towns. "I admire my mother because she received a college education, and she brought us this far with that education and salary," Brown says. "I know without my mother, my dad would be all weirded out. Nothing happens without my mother."

ʚ

My own mother, Dorothy—although my siblings and I are four grown adults—treats us as little children. When we come home to the reservation from the big cities, she greets us with enduring, affectionate greetings like *shiyazhi*, meaning "my little ones." She often butchers a sheep, Navajo-style, for the children who "ran off" to the cities. She also remembers our favorite parts of mutton. My sister Earlene loves

ribs. My older brother, Eisenhower, likes the soft part of the shoulder. My brother William eats everything, and my mother knows I like blood sausage and parts of roasted sheep head, like the tongue.

My young daughter Ninabah threatens to report her grandmother to animal-rights folks when my mother slaughters a goat or sheep. My citified daughter covers her eyes during this ritual or runs behind a sand dune. Ninabah says, "Ew, gross!" and watches us feast. This is not a time to watch our waistlines or be mindful of doctors' warnings.

On Sunday morning of the Western Navajo Nation Fair, when thousands of Navajos descend on Tuba City for their annual homecoming each fall, my mother makes tasty blood sausage with corn kernels, potatoes, a thick layer of sheep fat, and blood thickened with yellow cornmeal. She pours the waxy, bloody mixture into an empty sheep belly bag, tied at the end with a string and a small stick. She boils it to yummy perfection. I usually abscond with the ready-to-eat blood sausage from her stew pot, packing it in aluminum foil and a plastic bag.

My husband watches me, and as I proceed to walk toward his car, he stands in front of his car door. That's because the pungent aroma permeates everything, from cloth to plastic. He favors a "new car scent" in his Nissan city car. This year, we brought my Jeep, so I could pack the sausage in my vehicle and bring it home to Phoenix, saving his car from the penetrating scent.

Two weeks after one such fair, on a Sunday afternoon, I microwave a slice. I have forgotten how powerful the aroma can be. The smell is similar to tripe. My cats, Charlie and Wooshi, gasp for fresh air, howling at the front door to be let out. My kids unglue themselves from the boob tube and scramble outdoors.

"Mom, it's not Halloween!" my youngest daughter Ninabah says in protest before she marches out of the house. My husband, the chef of our home, renowned for delicious salsa and fresh chicken fajitas, quietly drives off to Home Depot.

I eat blood sausage in peace.

SOUTH

YOUNG ADULT

Tsoodził – Mount Taylor

COLETTE MARTINEZ'S BEAUTY BEGUILES PEOPLE. The tall young woman has delicate features and smooth brown skin framed by long dark hair that drapes to the small of her back, pointing to a pair of cowboy boots on her feet. There is a story behind those boots. Martinez, eighteen, is a true cowgirl at heart from Haystack, New Mexico, thirty miles west of Mount Taylor.

One doesn't leave Navajo Country without noticing bumper stickers about rodeos. When Colette's parents were young, Navajo cowboys were idolized, and weekend rodeos were favorite pastimes. Colette is a calf roper who graduated from Tohatchi High School. She rides steeds after calves at high speed. Colette understands that racing a horse after a calf while violently swishing a lasso in the air is considered a man's sport.

"Some men don't take me seriously, and they laugh about me because I'm a girl," she says. "They tell me, 'This is a man's sport.' Some girls get their feelings hurt, but I show enthusiasm about the sport, and I like to keep proving them wrong."

According to historians, horses were acquired by Navajos when Spaniards arrived in the Southwest. The Diné say livestock, like horses, were given to them as gifts by the Holy People.

Colette's mother has other plans for her daughter. She sent her to college, where she joined other Navajo women at Arizona State University. The pressure is intense among her family to have a first-generation college graduate. The freshman aspires to become a registered nurse, a career she selected as a ten-year-old when she visited Rehoboth McKinley Christian Health, a hospital in McKinley County. Colette remembers that there were few doctors and nurses to tend to ill patients. Careers in the field of health care are much sought after by the Navajo Nation's women, according to the tribe's scholarship records.

Her prayers to the Navajo Holy People are her foundation to cope with the rigors of a stressful college life. Colette belongs to Deeschii'nii (Start of the Red Streak Clan) and is born for Naakaii Dine'é (Mexican Clan). Although she did not learn to speak Navajo fluently as a child, she watches her mother journey to Mount Taylor for prayers. The parent clutches a bag of corn pollen and offers a pinch of the yellow powder, along with a prayer. Sometimes Colette accompanies her mother and quietly witnesses her mother's Navajo prayers.

Mothers could have taught the Navajo language to their children, but English became more dominant in their homes as many families moved into big cities or urban areas of the Nation. When a mother marries outside her race or to a Navajo spouse who does not speak the native tongue, English becomes the means of communication. Some mothers did not teach their children Navajo because they did not want them to struggle to communicate with the outside world. Flawless English was prized at one time. Navajo mothers who attended government-operated schools in the 1950s, 60s, and 70s left campuses as bilingual speakers. They were punished and shamed if they spoke Navajo, because the government was on a mission to assimilate them. Other bilingual mothers share experiences of how they were limited in opportunities for employment. Subsequently, they decided to spare their daughters from their own struggles.

Now there is a rebirth of desire among the youth to learn the language. Some Navajo mothers, to ensure their children grow up bilingual, encourage more interaction with their grandparents on the Nation when their daughters are young. Urban centers, such as the Phoenix Indian Center or the universities, also offer written and spoken Navajo language classes.

Colette hears plenty of spoken Navajo, but to engage in conversation she must be fluent. It is her goal to learn. "I can understand conversational Navajo, but I can't respond to my grandmother when she speaks," Colette says. "She calls me *jaa'ii* meaning 'no ears,' or I don't have the ears for the language."

Duties at the Haystack Rancho, a family-run ranch, taught Colette responsibility. Rodeo competition gave her the will to take risks. But she fears disappointing her family, especially if she fails to complete college. That's what drives her.

ত

Kristina Haskell grew up in Dilkon, north of Winslow, where the annual southern Navajo fair is celebrated in August. There, her grandparents raised her with the expectation that she would succeed, using modern education to charge into realms they never reached. Today, the thirty-year-old considers Phoenix home, where she bought a house and opened a business called Avalon Accounting.

The business shines in a corporate climate, far from the four sacred mountains surrounding the Navajo Nation, where clients hire her to straighten their financial books or to broker six-figure business deals. The most recent additions to her clients include Native American tribes.

At first glance, it's easy to assume the young woman is Latina. But she is of Navajo-Tewa descent, a single mother of two, who graduated from Arizona State University and serves on numerous service-oriented committees in Phoenix. She speaks English flawlessly and flirts with the idea of learning Spanish in order to attract customers from the country's fastest-growing minority population.

Haskell's pocket PC buzzes and twirls on a coffee table. She calms the noisy gadget after taking a quick glance and learns it's her office staff contacting her. In the Phoenix corporate world where Haskell conducts business, there are few American Indians. Her colleagues don't see her as a Navajo. They see her simply as a business woman. They are flabbergasted when she shares her background.

"People remark, 'You still exist?'" she says. The "you" refers to Native people.

Haskell, a brilliant, vivacious Navajo woman, is very aware of her roots. She belongs to Tó dích'íi'nii (Bitter Water Clan), and is born for the Hopi Tewa, or Bear Clan. Haskell believes it's her duty to represent Arizona's native people, whose legacy is often skewed in history books, and whose legacy is assumed to have vanished after the Wild West was settled. "We're here. We're professionals. We're smart. We're talented."

Haskell climbed to the crest of an accounting career from humble beginnings. Her grandparents deliberately chose not to teach her the Navajo language, because a Navajo accent could serve as a barrier to a prized American education.

"You'd better make something out of yourself," was drummed into Haskell by her grandparents.

Navajo grandparents raising their grandchildren on the Nation is a common and accepted practice, but Haskell is rekindling a relationship with her mother, who she says she is not close to. Haskell's mother spent many of her own early years away from the reservation in the Indian Student Placement Programs of the Church of Jesus Christ of Latter-day Saints. She was one of numerous Nation children who were paired up with Anglo Mormon families from Utah to California. When a middle-aged Navajo says "my foster mother or family," that generally means a church family off the reservation.

These programs were common in Navajo Country in the 1960s, 70s, and 80s before they ceased in 1990 because of mounting public criticism. The Indian Child Welfare Act of 1978, a federal law that restricted outright adoption of native children without a parent's consent, also conflicted with such programs. Before the act, some young Navajo children were sent off without a parent's consent or without much paperwork.

Haskell, a precocious child, also spent part of her childhood in Winslow, a town on the border of the Navajo Nation, twenty-four miles northeast of Dilkon. She learned about work ethics by watching her mother scrub toilets and make beds in hotel rooms, or fold towels in the laundry room. Haskell repeated the same manual jobs in high school and crammed working at two fast-food restaurants and a small accounting office into her busy high school life.

Advanced placement classes at school satisfied her hunger for knowledge. But there was a downside. Life at home was so unpleasant that it forced her into an apartment at age fifteen. She completed high school juggling three jobs without much family support. While hordes of extended Navajo families would show up to support a peer's accomplishment, like a play or graduation, her family, except for her grandmother, was absent.

She married an Anglo corrections officer, and they later divorced. Her grandmother is now raising her two young children while Haskell builds her business, which requires attention twenty-four hours a day, seven days a week. She would like her children to learn the Navajo language, which will be more likely while they are living with her grandmother.

In hindsight, Haskell concludes, "Being a trailblazer, it's very lonely."

Her future goal is to form a nonprofit business organization that serves as a support group for Native Americans in the city. Haskell also envisions her children living with her once her business reaches a milestone and generates a strong steady income.

I did not feel one bit like Changing Woman that hot August day. The only cool spot on the western Navajo Nation was a cat's nose. That was the day I ran as a kinaalda, reenacting Changing Woman's run when she received her first menses. The women in my family imposed taboos forbidding me to smile, giggle, or consume sweets, because my body is changing. A smile or giggle would unleash wrinkles. Sweets decayed teeth. They told me Changing Woman ran east and west for four days to build endurance and then ground corn on a metate.

My family had camped near Yaanidee'nil, Where the Mesas Clump Together, just above a deep gully that crisscrossed and plunged into the Little Colorado River gorge. I had jogged too far away from our camp. I glanced at the dirt road that meandered up the butte. Another dirt road darted off to the west, leading to the flat area where my family camped. There sat my grandmother Edith's camp, consisting of my father's hogan. My grandmother's canvas tent sat next to an arbor. Nearby was a pen for the flock of sheep.

I wore a Navajo outfit composed of a maroon-colored velveteen shirt, a three-tiered pink silk skirt, a sash, and jewelry. A strand of buckskin held my jet-black hair in a ponytail. The weight of turquoise and silver sapped my energy beneath the intense heat. I heard my mother's strand of turquoise beads tap on my father's two-pound silver belt wrapped around my waist. My leg muscles burned. Pebbles stung my feet because of the thin soles of my moccasins. Beads of perspiration dribbled down my face.

Two days before this run, I had played with my collection of rock toys in a clump of sagebrush. Long skinny rocks were women, and sticks turned to men. Tiny pebbles collected from a wash were sheep. An empty rusty-colored sardine can served as a vehicle.

I panicked when I learned I had become a kinaalda. I shared the news with my mother, who told my grandmother, who insisted on a ceremony. My mother instructed me that day to walk away from my toys in the sagebrush.

"You are now an adult," she told me.

I regretted sharing the news with my mother, because I now had a challenge before me: to jog half a mile up the butte in the heat, weighted down by jewelry and bad shoes. My pesky brother William and cousins Egbert, Hubert, Robert, and Nelson zoomed past me at record speed. Hubert, in an attempt to fashion a show-and-tell, raced to the top of the mesa, threw pebbles for entertainment, ran down to the bottom of the butte, and shot past me once more.

I remembered my grandmother's words: "Let them run past you. They are forbidden to outrun a kinaalda. They will age before you."

I completed that run just short of tears. Decades later, I continue to monitor my cousin Hubert's face for wrinkles.

DOORWAY

BETWEEN TRADITIONAL & MODERN LIFE

SHEILA GOLDTOOTH AND REBECCA M. BENALLY are examples of Navajo women who blend the American and Navajo philosophies to carry out their work. Their careers and professions influence Navajo life and represent the merging of traditional and contemporary practices occurring through the doorway of the Nation. Navajo medicine people are keepers of the wisdom, traditional faith, and philosophy of iiná—life—on the Nation. Educators inspire children to pursue modern knowledge.

When Sheila Goldtooth had her kinaalda, a Navajo girl's rite of passage, her uncle performed the Hózhóójí, or Blessing Way, a ritual performed to ensure a blessed life of good health, emotional strength, prosperity, and a positive outlook. Goldtooth's uncle announced, "*Díí beebi'dool zíí*," meaning: "This one has a gift."

Dawn peeked over the Chuska Mountains, near Tsénikani, or Round Rock, as Goldtooth's kinaalda was near completion. The tiny community is located a stone's throw from Monument Valley, an area famous for its red buttes and rock spires that sit on the desert floor and reach toward blue skies.

"*Díí Hózhóójí doo náałhaashda* (This one will be a Blessing Way singer)," the uncle said. "*Dii bidine' éyíká adoolwol* (This one will help her people)."

Those words sealed Goldtooth's fate to pursue a profession rare among Navajo women. She has become a medicine woman. They call her Hataałi Bitsií lichíí', the Medicine Woman with the Red Hair. She belongs to the Ma'ii deeshgiizhnii (Coyote Pass People) and is born for Kin lichíi'nii (Red House People). The educator at Diné Community College in Tsaile-Wheatfields has trailed her uncle since age five. Today, Navajos seek out the thirty-year-old to bless their lives between Yádiłhił Shitaá (Father Sky) and Shimá Nahasdzáán (Mother Earth).

When they journey outside the four sacred mountains—relocation to the city, college, or a job site—Navajos come to Goldtooth to bless their forays. They

also seek a blessing before surgery, before they move into a new home, or when a girl becomes a kinaalda.

The kinaalda, a four-day ceremony, reflects Changing Woman's first ritual when the Navajo Holy People gathered on Huerfano Mountain in New Mexico. Oral history says the Navajo deities treat this moment in the young girl's life as pure, powerful, and sacred. It is said Changing Woman jogged east and west to gain physical strength and endurance. Medicine people say the Holy People performed the first Hózhóójí. Changing Woman ground corn kernels on a metate stone, a round corn cake was baked in the earth, and a female holy person physically shaped and molded Changing Woman's body by pressing her head, shoulders, arms, back, legs, and feet.

The kinaalda creates a reenactment of how the Navajo Holy People held the rite of passage for Changing Woman. She was dressed and painted in white shell and received a second name, Yoołgai Azdáá (White Shell Woman). The old belief says that this is when adulthood and procreation begins for Navajo women. Today, most Navajo women are aware of the American stages of life, beginning as a baby, progressing to adolescence, adulthood, and old age. The contemporary kinaalda ritual varies and depends on the energy of relatives, cost, and time. Navajo families on an American work schedule may condense the event into a single night on a weekend. They skip certain rituals such as the four-day run, or they opt to have the Blessing Way only, without the elaborate ritual. Other mothers replace the physically laborious creation of the ground corn cake with a slab of chocolate cake from a supermarket.

Navajos say their deities gave them other curing rituals such as the Lifeway (Iináájí k'ehgo) and Female Shooting Way (Na'at'ooyee' Bi'áádjí), and seasonal ceremonies such as the Enemy Way (Anaa'jí), before they faded into the mountains, rocks, water, and vegetation. Navajo medicine people call on the Holy People, who are believed to attend the Blessing Way, seasonal ceremonies, and curing rituals. The Blessing Way is said to be associated with Navajo women.

Medicine people like Goldtooth, called *hataałii*, which translates to "singers" in English, are trained by elders to perfect them in the skills of their profession. So when Goldtooth received her *jish*, or medicine bundle, which holds a powerful collection of tools, her connection to Navajo Country also deepened.

"I feel that in order to serve people, I need to be here," Goldtooth remarks. "I grew up here. I have a flock of sheep. It's that serenity of life here that suits me and what I do for my people. I lived in Flagstaff. It's too noisy, polluted. The ceremonies are connected to the land here."

Goldtooth attended Northern Arizona University, where she received Western knowledge culminating in a bachelor degree in Native American studies and sociology. A Western education could have guided her away from the four sacred mountains and into a border town or city where jobs are available. Instead, she returned to Round Rock to continue her role as a Blessing Way hataalii and also to perform protection prayers.

Not all Navajos embrace traditional worship. Other faiths are available, ranging from Christian to the Native American Church, a worship that blends traditional Navajo religion and Christianity beliefs with the use of peyote. Some Navajos hopscotch between faiths. Detractors from the traditional Navajo faith cite cost and a lack of access to medicine people. Others blame the American life that forces them to move into the city for jobs. Subsequently, they lose ties with extended family relatives whose energy and resources are needed to pull off a successful ceremony. Many Navajo youth are born into other faiths, which their parents embrace and encourage.

Traditional Navajo faith also rides on the oral language. When medicine people such as Goldtooth call on the Holy People to bless an individual during

a prayer, each deity carries a name. To receive a blessing or help, the correct enunciation is required. Goldtooth notices more Navajo children speak only English, which forces medicine people like herself to modify their work. Sometimes mothers recite the prayers in Navajo for their daughters. Goldtooth places the responsibility on the girls.

"I explain [in English] that the Holy People only understand Navajo, and therefore everything must be done in that language. I make them do their own reciting in prayers rather than having a parent do the reciting. I explain how the prayer is for them and their future, and therefore they must do them themselves." And it works. By the time the ceremony ends, most of the daughters are able to repeat the prayer in Navajo.

The medicine woman also notices that change occurs when Navajo youth move into urban Navajo communities or off the Nation. As a result, Goldtooth believes that urban life erodes Navajo language and philosophy, especially the influence it has on a child's behavior. This includes respect for parents, elders, and other people. Navajo children are taught in the Navajo language to never speak harsh words, because they can inflict pain. But Western instruction encourages youth to speak up and have an opinion—to be argumentative and to solve problems through an analytical process is prized in the American society. The traditional ability to solve issues with *k'é*, in the spirit of good and harmony, is gone.

"I find that with my students at the community college," Goldtooth says. "Their attitude is, that is in the past. We don't need it anymore. They also say, if it [Diné teachings] is true, then there has to be proof."

The survival of Navajo religion and philosophy depends on parents' teaching the language, stories, rituals, and philosophy. Still, that may not be enough. "If the Navajo Nation leaders become actively involved in preserving and passing laws regarding preservation of our traditional healing methods and ceremonies, they can be preserved," Goldtooth states. "There are numerous young traditional practitioners throughout the Navajo Nation, and [yet] many are unknown to the public."

ʊ

When Navajo educator Rebecca M. Benally took the helm of the Montezuma Creek Elementary School in the northern portion of the Navajo Nation in Utah, the new staff disapproved of her promotion to principal. They did not object to her wealth of experience in the education field, but to her gender. What shocked Benally even more was the attitude that masked the resistance by Navajo educators—especially female educators.

Montezuma Creek is an isolated Navajo community, surrounded by red buttes, in which a trip to a "local" grocery store means a 110-mile drive (one way) to Farmington, New Mexico. Christian missionaries in the 1920s attempted to tame the wild surroundings, but even today the local Aneth Chapter House, one of 110 communities on the Navajo Nation, is wedged in an arroyo. The influence of missionaries spurred an exodus of children to off-reservation schools and introduced the concept of a male-dominated society, in which men were "head of household" and made all the important decisions.

So when Benally arrived, she was soon approached by a Navajo colleague who confided that her Mormon faith made it uncomfortable to work in a setting where a woman was in charge. A clash of cultures seemed certain, because the Navajo culture is both matrilineal and matriarchal, while the Mormon-dominated community of Montezuma Creek promotes a patrilineal society. Benally, who belongs to the Kin yaa'áanii (Towering House People) and is born for Tó 'aheedlíinii (Two Rivers Coming Together Clan), found herself in a difficult spot.

The elementary school staff expected the Navajo educator to throw up her arms in defeat and walk away from criticism, as was traditional when change was suggested in the school community. The workers did not realize that this Navajo educator knew more about them than they did about her, and she refused to wilt under pressure. She was on a mission to raise student test scores in order to pass the federal report card and to move Navajo kids out of special education.

Benally refused to give in. She had come too far to make accommodations. For two summers, she had driven 608 miles (round trip) three times a week from Montezuma Creek to Provo, Utah, while working on a master's degree in educational leadership. She took a hard line and told those who opposed her leadership because of her gender they could leave, if they wished.

The stance resulted in an exodus of those resistant to female leadership. Then, something almost miraculous happened. When she first arrived on campus, half of the 210 students were in special education classes. The teachers who remained under her leadership focused on 105 children, moving twenty-one of them into regular classrooms, where they thrived, within the first year. Today, fewer than twenty students are in special education at Montezuma Creek.

Local leaders told Benally that "Navajos can be like crabs in a bucket." When one tries to get out, they pull each other back. "I always stood for the betterment of Navajo children," she says. Having to face a battle over gender in educational leadership was a distraction.

"The two reasons students were automatically placed in the special education program was simply for language development acquisition and a lack of knowledge to work with children with learning disabilities," Benally notes. "My drive to overcome obstacles and challenges is always for the betterment and best interest for *all* children. I believe we should all be advocates for children."

Benally is among those Navajos who delicately integrate both traditional Navajo cultural values and teachings and Western philosophy. As a Navajo woman, she maintains a Beauty Way of life. Both her father and grandfather had encouraged Benally to remember that her role as a woman meant that she was responsible for the passing down of cultural knowledge from mother to daughter, and for setting a good example that provides an important balance to the words and actions of men, resulting in Navajo harmony between traditional and contemporary life.

To be a Navajo woman means connecting the spiritual, intellectual, social, and the physical. At school, this meant accepting both the role of being a woman and being a leader in education—reconciling the two, never subjugating herself in the process.

Encouraging her to excel in school, her father instructed Benally at an early age that she would have to overcome the male domination of the larger world. "You are a Navajo woman in a white man's world," he told her. "Never forget who you are and where you come from."

Going against the grain would be difficult, and Benally would need to summon the strength of her cultural upbringing to succeed. In the field of Western education, questioning authority is encouraged, however, and harmony often is more difficult to achieve. This was the case when she began her new role as a school principal, again remembering her father's words: "Be competitive with elegance." Benally says she succeeds by taking the best of both worlds and applying them in her job.

"A medicine man told me, 'For every bad thing that happens, there is a way to fix it. It is fixed with corn pollen and positive thoughts.'" She says she prays to the Holy People.

Culture and academic learning become one, and Aneth's students—most of whom are Navajo—learn how to apply what they have learned at school to their lives on the reservation and globally. Benally wanted to influence the Navajo Nation's curriculum further and campaigned for a seat on the first Navajo Nation Board of Education. She won.

Yuhzhee is my Navajo name. It translates as "short" or "petite" in English. At age seven, I spoke only Navajo. My family, simple shepherds and part-time migrant workers, raised and moved their flock of sheep at a place called Bidáá, on the northeastern edge of the Grand Canyon. Bidáá means, simply, "The Edge."

While the rest of America paid attention to the Vietnam War and the civil rights movement, my extended family focused its attention on existence. Rain, snow, sunshine, or wind, they took the sheep out to pasture.

Our religion—Hózhóó, or Beauty—demands balance, which holds my extended family like a tight weave in a Navajo rug. This faith, embedded like stone into our young Navajo hearts, minds, and souls, protects us. Iiná, life, we were told by our elders, is full of bad and evil. And to fend off the bad, Hózhóó helped us to think positive.

As a Navajo child, I believed my life was rich, because I had plenty of relatives, sheep, and religion. The women and my father who raised me never

learned to recite the ABCs or read classic literature, like Shakespeare. From their flock of sheep, they wove pretty rugs. They sold sheep to buy potatoes, lard, baking powder, salt, and coffee. Or they made payments on a communal pickup truck. They turned to migrant work in the summer, pulling sugar beets in Utah. Out of their work, Navajos coined the phrase *Áshii łikantah*, or "Among Sugar Land." Sometimes I joined in picking the potatoes in Elsinore, Utah.

The price of wool and mohair took a nosedive in the 1980s. Our family reduced the herd from 500 to twenty-one. Today, my mother and her sister-in-law Jeanette are retired shepherds who live in Tuba City, closer to clinics and hospitals. Others, like my grandmother Edith, my aunt Lutie, and my father, Willie, returned to the earth.

My brother William, a biology teacher at Tuba City High School and my mother's caregiver, continues to care for the tiny flock of sheep that belongs to my family near Bidáá, west of Tuba City. My mother likes this arrangement, because she believes the sheep give her life, which is how they are described in Navajo prayers. The sheep ground her to the traditional elements of the Navajo Nation.

This is my family's glorious past as Navajo shepherds.

CATS

WEST

ADULTHOOD

Dook'o'oosłííd – San Francisco Peaks

VANESSA WAUNEKA DOES NOT WANT TO LEAVE her mother alone on the Navajo Nation. Her mother is in good health. In fact, she continues to work as an educator. Still, Wauneka, thirty-two, believes it's her duty to look after her mother, a widow. Daily visits and twice-a-day telephone conversations are the norm.

"I fear losing my mother because she's a big part of my life," says Wauneka, a cashier at the historic Tuba City Trading Post. "I think it's easier to live on the rez. I see my siblings experience financial difficulty. Everything seems to be about money if you live in the city."

Living in Tuba City requires Wauneka to speak fluent Navajo, because many of her customers are elders who speak only Navajo. Too many Tuba City youth speak only English. "The young kids are too cool to know things of their heritage," Wauneka notes.

She believes living in Tuba City benefits her son, who will grow up knowing his grandmother, who calls him *shitsóí*, grandson. The young Tuba City resident is from the Áshiihí (Salt Clan), and is born for the Zuni Edge People, or Naasht'ézhí Dine'é Tábaahí.

Navajo mothers bug their daughters at all stages of life. Some moms assign a million chores and expect them to be completed in one second. Other mothers are nostalgic about the old days when they grew up on the reservation in houses without running water or television, and woke at dawn for chores after a night of sleeping under the stars. Some have other quirks.

Wauneka believes her mother wants a perfect daughter. Her mother spent time in Oakland, California, in college during the 1960s. She moved there after attending Albuquerque Indian School, a Bureau of Indian Affairs school where thousands of young Navajos received their elementary and high school education. She met Wauneka's father at the Albuquerque school. They married in the late 60s when they moved back to the Nation after Wauneka's father completed a tour in Vietnam as a marine. Wauneka's mother is an educator, and her dad was a tribal police officer and cultural instructor in Tuba City.

"My mother tries to control my thoughts and my life," Wauneka remarks. "I have to get things right the first time. For example, my son likes to play games. She tells me, 'You should let him color.' With my siblings, she doesn't control their lives like she does mine."

When she feels smothered by her mother, Wauneka yearns to move away from Tuba City. The urge is so strong that she enrolled at Diné Community College in Tuba City to find out what higher education entailed. She took English and algebra and is now working to receive a liberal arts associate degree.

The single mother is the daughter who stayed behind while her five siblings moved into big cities and became urban Navajos. They all finished high school, but a lack of jobs on the Nation forced them off the reservation. Like clockwork, they return home to celebrate holidays such as Christmas, birthdays, or the Tuba City Fair. They seem to lead harried lives in the city and worry about bills.

"I think it costs a lot of money to live in the city, because that's all my siblings talk about when they visit," Wauneka says. "I feel lucky living in Tuba City when I hear them discuss their bills."

Wauneka appears timid at first but is chatty and friendly, a personality also suitable for the tourists who visit Tuba City. She previously worked the register at a grocery store. By the time her son celebrates his thirty-first birthday in twenty years, Wauneka predicts the Navajo Nation will be more modern and there will be continued movement into cities, where she predicts her son will live.

A decade ago, Marilyn McReeves also wanted to live "out there" off the Nation and in a big city, like Wauneka's siblings. But that wasn't meant to be. She's been a Nation resident for all but two of her forty-four years. She belongs to the Tsé deeshgizhnii (Rock Gap Clan), and is born for the Tł'ááshchí'í (Red Bottom People).

McReeves, a mother of four, is articulate. She manages the Navajo Nation Arts & Crafts Enterprise, the Nation's largest nonprofit organization. She attended one semester of high school in Chicago, worked for the Navajo Nation Police Department as a dispatcher after graduating from Tuba City's Greyhills High School, and received her associate degree from Haskell Junior College in Kansas.

Cameron, a tiny community situated between the Grand Canyon and the Little Colorado River, lies forty miles north of Flagstaff on Highway 89. The enterprise McReeves manages thrives from sales to tourists on their way to the Grand Canyon and sales to urban Navajos from Phoenix hankering for jewelry.

"I've tried moving away from Cameron, but my mom draws me back," McReeves says. "She was a mom and dad to me when I was little."

Her mother, with just a sixth-grade education, and the community are ties she can't bear to walk away from. As a manager, she meets numerous customers and Navajo artists. McReeves beams when an elderly Navajo woman brings in a hand-woven rug to sell. The ladies greet her as though she were their child and call her *shich'é'é*, or daughter.

"Everything is so impersonal in the city," McReeves states. "I can tell how the city changes a person. Urban Navajos are usually frazzled, in a hurry, and say stuff without thinking. They put you down. Maybe that is called being direct out there in the outside world. They come across as rude and superior here."

But McReeves is not one to wilt. She is aware of the American feminist struggles and sees things from a woman's eye. Those eyes have seen plenty. About the time she completed high school, the federal government marked boundaries on the former Navajo-Hopi joint-use area. The boundary is a ninety-minute drive northeast from Cameron on a paved road. She followed news accounts about how the federal government relocated 10,000 Navajos off land awarded to the neighboring Hopi tribe. Congress divided nearly two million acres of joint-use area land equally between the two tribes in 1974. Navajos had settled the entire area, and subsequently the federal government relocated them off lands where they had been raised. Many Navajo families complied and moved into cities or urban areas of the Navajo Nation. Others, particularly a group of Navajo women, refused. These women became icons of resistance.

McReeves admires Navajo women such as Pauline Whitesinger, Catherine Smith, and the late Roberta Blackgoat as heroes, role models, and leaders who stood up to the federal government and questioned why they had to move away from their ancestral land. It causes McReeves to reflect about Navajo women in her own extended family.

McReeves grew up attending the Assembly of God Church in the 1960s and 70s, listening to Fleetwood Mac and the late Waylon Jennings, and cruising reservation roads in pickup trucks outfitted with CB radios. It was a time in Navajo history when few Navajos were brave enough to march onto college campuses.

Perhaps the flighty urge to leave the Nation arose when her mother's friend from Chicago invited McReeves to live with her and attend high school in

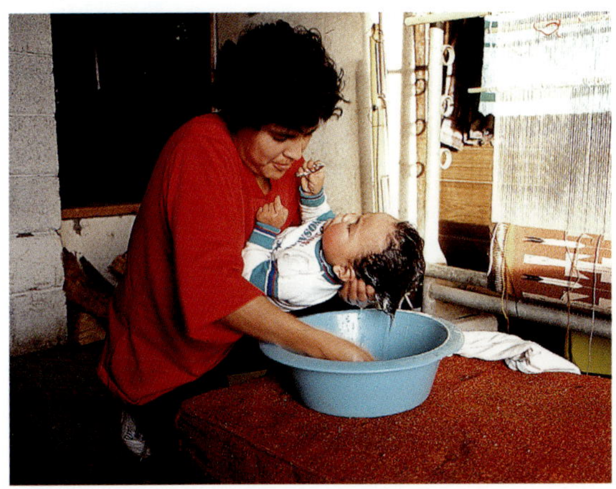

Illinois. It gave her a taste of life away from the reservation and the boarding schools. Years earlier, in 1966, a uranium mine exploded in Milford, Utah. It left McReeves's mother a widow with eight young children to raise. Her mother collected the kids and moved home to Cameron, on the western edge of the Navajo Nation. She enrolled her children in Tuba City Boarding School, thirty miles northeast of Cameron, in a Bureau of Indian Affairs residential dorm and school. A young McReeves walked into the tan residential building with orange stripes. There the government school taught her how to be an American. She enjoyed learning, but the residential dorm aides were like generals with their discipline practices. In hindsight, the school functioned very much like a military operation, where Navajo students were told their language was forbidden and where they were kept busy scrubbing the residential hall.

When she returned home from Tuba City Boarding School to see her mother on the weekends, McReeves spent time running after sheep, while her mother kept the family financially afloat with jewelry work. Sometimes she wonders how her mom raised eight kids on the Nation and watched them all become adults. Her mother's generation grew up with a philosophy of, "the more children one had, the wealthier you were."

McReeves, however, applied American economics to the number of children she had. "It's that American dollar," she says. "But I consider Navajo women to be strong-minded, and when there is a crisis the women in my family move to the forefront and solve issues. I see it at my store. When a Navajo woman brings in a jewelry piece or a rug, they approach me [to initiate a conversation about selling their artwork], while the men drop to the background. I always thought that odd."

ʘ

My sister Earlene calls from Salt Lake City, Utah. She complains about her daughters. She whines, "They won't pick up after themselves!" A piece of paper will stay on the floor for a month and no one picks it up, she tells me. "Until I get upset, people just lay there. They don't move until I get mad at them."

I glance at my daughter Ninabah's messy room: unmade beds, stuffed animals strewn on the floor, pants piled into a corner, T-shirts heaped in the middle of the floor, and drawers pulled out of her dresser. A stale air freshener dangles from the ceiling. I can relate to my sister's frustrations. My daughters, Ninabah and JJ, justify their poor housekeeping by creating their own definition of what is a clean room.

"It's not that military cleaning that you and Earlene were taught at the federal boarding school," my older daughter, JJ, says. She now lives in a university dormitory where anything goes.

Earlene and I continue to carry on about our five daughters—JJ, Bianica, Rudilynn, Veronica, and Ninabah. All are adults except Ninabah. A question we often raise with the girls is this: "Who will clean after you when you get your own apartment?"

Our chatter shifts to when we were living in boarding schools on the Navajo Nation and elsewhere in the 1960s and 70s. We shoot the breeze about our guilt, living today in the city while our elderly mother lives on the Nation. Our justification is

this: We have mortgages and bills to pay. There are zero jobs on the reservation.

Before we hit our teenage years, we cleaned hotel rooms and folded sheets and towels at Page Boy Motel in the closest border community of Page, Arizona, about sixty miles north from Bodaway, our home on the reservation. Sometimes on summer nights we slept in the bed of my father's light blue Ford truck beneath brilliant stars just outside of the city limits.

Years before we started working in Page, my sister Earlene and I formed a pact while our sheepherding family was camping in a large gully known to my family as Tsa' Tah, or Among the Sagebrush. To the world, it was a stone's throw from the confluence of the Colorado River and the Little Colorado River, but to Earlene and me it was home. The pact was that I would learn to read and write English and help Earlene. My sister is a single mother and has only a second-grade education. She helped our parents tend to the flock of sheep, and later with financial help, while she worked as a dishwasher at a public school. Earlene (named Tsisigo, which means The Small One in Navajo) stood up to my grandmother, because she wanted me to have what she didn't have—an education. In turn, I felt an obligation to help her with English.

Earlene had clipped a section of the *Navajo Times* with a picture and a mailing address of a soldier in Vietnam. I must have been in third grade, learning how to write letters at Tuba City Boarding School. It started with writing letters for her to soldiers in Vietnam. I wrote simple letters about the weather at Sagebrush and asked a lot of questions. I'm not sure if the soldiers ever responded.

Later, it turned to writing notes to her children's teachers or her bosses in Salt Lake City. It also entailed reading her mail when her kids were small. Today Earlene remains challenged when speaking or reading English. So when health ailments develop, she calls me to translate medical terms. I admire my big sister, because she single-handedly raised three daughters whose father died before they stepped into preschool. She juggles three jobs and manages to stay calm.

We decide our efforts to analyze why our daughters are not great housekeepers are minor compared to big issues looming ahead of us. There is the care of our mother and a brother with multiple sclerosis, and another brother currently caring for our mother and, of course, our own health.

We end our telephone conversation, optimistic that in our old age, our own daughters will embrace the Navajo philosophy of children caring for their elders. We are Navajo sáanii full of wisdom and moving toward elder stage, but we are challenged when we try to share our philosophy with our daughters who, unlike us, grew up in an Americanized world. We communicate better with each other and with other Navajos of our generation and with similar backgrounds.

163
104
539

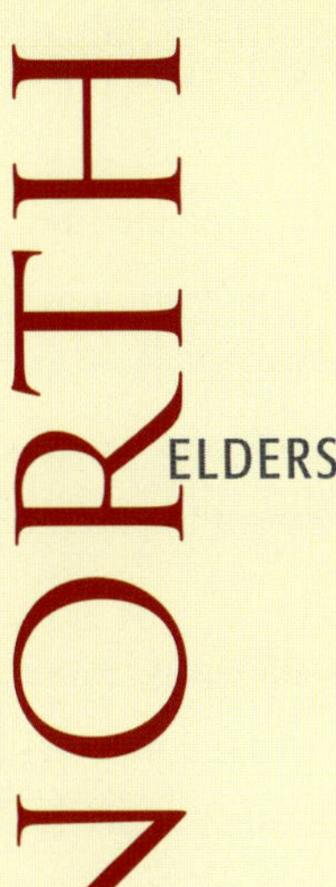

NORTH ELDERS

Dibé Nitsaa – Mount Hesperus

IF YOU DIVIDED THE NAVAJO NATION into quadrants, Navajo Mountain would be at the top of the world to the Navajo Nation. The mountain sits at 10,416 feet above sea level and is the northern border of the Nation, though it is considered to be in the western Navajo region. Navajos know the mountain as Naatsis'áán, or the Head of the Earth. The 636-member community that lives nearby straddles the Arizona-Utah border, along scenic Lake Powell. At the northwestern foot of the mountain stands the famous Rainbow Bridge.

Arizona political icon Barry Goldwater once flew around the mountain in the 1940s, when he owned a trading post here. This was his playground. But to the Navajo people, Navajo Mountain is Tádídíín Dzil, or Corn Pollen Mountain. Local residents and Goldwater have one thing in common: an independent streak. Navajos share stories about how they survived the frigid winters or shoveled their way out of this isolated community when bad snowstorms hit. A portion of its major southern access road was paved in the 1990s.

Jean Marie Holgate lives in the shadow of Navajo Mountain, on its eastern side, at the end of a gravel road. She belongs to the Tó dích'íi'nii (Bitter Water Clan) and is born for Táchii'nii (Red Running into Water Clan). An old, white Dodge is parked beside the house, and each morning Holgate boards the old pickup to head to Navajo Mountain Community School, where she works as a janitor. She sees a changing Navajo society unfold before her daily at her work. But on the weekends, Holgate, fifty-nine, continues to run a flock of sheep through the sagebrush and patches of juniper trees that dot the otherwise barren and windswept mesas.

"I was married once, but he left," Holgate says, standing on a mesa. She raised four children on her own. "My mom once said, 'She will be the one who takes care of the sheep, cards the wool, and weaves rugs.'" And that is why Holgate never went to *ólta'*, or school. Ever.

Holgate remembers at age six waking up before dawn, at 4 a.m., to grind corn. Potatoes, corn, tortillas, and frequently mutton were staples of the

diet—eaten for breakfast, lunch, and dinner. She comes from a family of nine, the sixth child, caring for younger siblings but not old enough to hold a major decision-making role. She learned how to weave sumac into the traditional Navajo wedding basket, which is given away when a daughter is married. The tan, red, and black circular basket is also sold to collectors or to trading posts, which thrive as the place to socialize or pick up supplies or mail on the Nation.

Her mother once said, "You must be artistic—have a talent—weave or make a pot." She said that talent will help you feed and clothe your children. She also said, "*Tááhwóájít' éegot'éiya,*" or it is Holgate's responsibility to shape her iiná, her life. So that is what Holgate did, as had many generations before her.

Holgate drifted from her traditional Navajo culture thirty years ago to join the Navajo Alliance Church, part of the Assemblies of God denomination. She says a local community member evangelized and converted many members of Navajo Mountain. When work and livestock duties ebb, Holgate attends Bible camps and Sunday worship.

On the weekends, Holgate takes her sheep out to graze. Only now, this is not part of daily life, rather a recreational pastime—a break from her janitor duties. "You have to wake up early and get to work," Holgate says, remembering the words of her parents. "Don't sleep too late, or your children will starve." Such was the case in the days of her grandparents, when every minute counted towards survival.

But like others of Holgate's generation, she sent her four children to Westernized schools so that they would not have to live a similar life. One son is a minister in Omaha, Nebraska; two sons work in construction and live outside the Nation. The fourth, her daughter, attends Prescott College, determined to remain single until she finishes college. Holgate is proud of her children's accomplishments. Her daughter visits her frequently and helps her sort mail, but she does not herd sheep as her ancestors did.

Navajos were orators in Holgate's younger days. When elders spoke, Navajo youth listened and respected their words of wisdom. Today, Holgate sees a generation of Navajo youth who lack knowledge about their roots and who they are. Sometimes the schools enlist her to speak to students about her past. But few, if any, lectures sink in, because many children carry a bad attitude and sport *ee'lihinii*, or black clothing.

"You can't tell who the women are anymore," Holgate complains. "Female students at the community school wear big, floppy, black jeans and cannot be distinguished from the guys. I ask them, 'Whose children are you?'" The girls shrug.

Holgate has made them part of a new twenty-first-century Navajo clan, which she dubs the "You-Nudge-Your-Shoulder Clan."

Holgate continues to dress in a skirt with a cotton shirt, just like her mother. She notices fewer Navajo women wear what she considers simple, classic traditional attire. When graduation ceremonies are held, though, families dig out pretty velveteen shirts and multitiered silk skirts for the young women.

What keeps Holgate strong as a Navajo woman is her adherence to her traditional upbringing and the Bible-based church. She speaks little English, coping with work at the school by relying on interpreters. Holgate and her brothers and sisters were raised in the outskirts of Navajo Mountain as shepherds. That lifestyle barely lasted four generations. Her children have no longing for the same lifestyle.

"In my mind, I don't see my children coming back to Navajo Mountain," Holgate says. She sees her daughter living in the big city. But Holgate keeps the sheep anyway, hoping the youngest child, her daughter, might still return someday.

ʘ

Sarah H. Natani's clan is Many Hogans, Hooghan Lání, and she is born for the Mexican Clan, Naakaii' Dine'é. Her modern octagonal hogan in Table Mesa lies thirteen miles south of Shiprock, a large agricultural community on the San Juan River, twenty miles west of the Navajo Nation border at Farmington, New Mexico. In the border-town environment, where Navajo culture mixes and clashes with that of the white man, tribal affiliation and where you were raised connects Navajo members.

Natani hears fewer Navajo children speaking the Navajo language, *Diné bizaad.* Instead, young children chatter in English. When a Navajo child is born in a modern hospital today, for example, the baby hears the English words, "It's a girl!" or "It's a boy!"

Natani, a retired weaver and instructor, predicts that the Navajo language will decline in the next generation. "We'll turn into a nation that speaks English only, and our kids will turn into *bilagonas* (Anglos), and they will fully accept the American lifestyle, the values," Natani remarks. "My elders used to tell me our ability to speak Diné bizaad defines us."

The Navajo language is so powerful that, when used to address relatives during an introduction, it connects one's identity by clans. Tell a group of Navajos your mother's clan is Tl'izilani (Manygoats Clan), and you can expect to gain instant mothers, aunts, brothers, sisters, or grandparents.

The seventy-year-old elder says the clan ties create k'é, a Navajo extended family terminology that promotes a peaceful and respectful relationship between families or neighbors. This is how large extended Navajo families live and thrive together. The extended clan system has an embedded force to control disputes or calm quarrels.

"Today, we call people next door our neighbors," Natani says. "It's too impersonal. In my generation, we identified each other as *shi'mayazhi*, my aunt, or *shi'dai*, my uncle, and *shi'ma'saani*, my maternal grandmother, or *shi'nali*, my paternal grandfather."

Natani, after seven decades of life on the Nation, has seen much change in Navajo society. The mother, grandmother, and great-grandmother admits that she and her late husband decided against teaching the Navajo language to four of their six children when they were young.

"We did not want them to struggle with the English language like we did," Natani says. "We could not speak Navajo in the city. We used the language well on the Navajo reservation, but our kids' future was outside of Navajo. My youngest daughter, who spoke English only, joined the Navy and is taking classes to learn to speak Navajo. Now she wants me to speak to my granddaughter in Navajo."

In hindsight, the elder understands the power of the language. The spoken word is strong because it has curative powers, especially when it is uttered in a prayer or in a Blessing Way song from the mouths of medicine people, such as Sheila Goldtooth. The spoken Navajo word is so powerful that the United States military enlisted Navajos to use the language in a military code. The code was used to confound the Japanese enemy during World War II and help win the war.

Natani was born in 1937 near the place Navajos call Tsé alnaozt'i'í (Crisscrossing Boulders), or Sanostee, New Mexico. Her father designed saddles and bridles for horsemen in the 1940s, and her mother made pottery and tended a flock of sheep.

"A woman's place was at the home, and my mother cared for the herd," Natani recalls. "School was secondary, because my mother needed my help with the flock."

Natani's parents raised nine children, who roamed between Sanostee and Upper Fruitland, New Mexico, her father's birthplace. The family picked berries and potatoes on the edge of the San Juan River before the large body of water was diverted to nearby irrigation fields. In 1949, Natani attended the U.S. government's education program for older native students, which she later learned was aimed at assimilating tribes. After attending this camp school, Natani relocated to the Sherman Institute in California to train to be a nurse. Illness hindered her from finishing a five-year program, and she returned to Sanostee.

"I think what they (the government) wanted us to do was to go to the city and become urban Indians through the program," Natani recalls. "We were supposed to vanish into big cities. It didn't happen. Today, the federal government, I think, dislikes us because we cost more money to be looked after, although they signed contracts to do so."

When Natani speaks about agreements, she is referring to historical treaties signed by Congress and the American Indian tribes. These contracts were agreed upon to deal with land and resources the nations lost through war and relocation of tribes during conflicts. Many tribes were moved to reservations. After freeing the Navajos from Bosque

Redondo in 1868, the government returned the Navajos to their country. Nation members agreed to put down their arms, and the government signed a treaty promising free public safety, education, and health care. Subsequently, Congress has imposed varied changes to the treaties over the years. For example, the Eisenhower administration erased a number of tribes—eliminating their recognition and rights initially promised by the treaties.

Back home in the 1960s, Natani waitressed at a Shiprock restaurant, married, and raised children. She and her late husband, a carpenter and tribal employee, spent their golden years traveling and lecturing about Navajo weaving. Tending sheep is no longer a part of the family's lifestyle, but memories of it endure.

"During lambing season on cold winter nights, we tied ewes and baby lambs near the hogan entrance so they would not freeze to death. My mother would build a fire in a wood-burning stove to keep them warm," she says. "No one said that sheep stink. Today, my daughter tells me, 'Mutton stinks.'"

ɕ

I remember my life as a child and the Navajo creation stories my father told and the adventures of Coyote. I remember living in hogans with roofs of thatched mud in the winter and living in simple canvas tents in the summer. The high winds shook the fabric—a comforting experience because we knew The Wind People, Navajo deities, were checking in on us.

I remember chubby lambs in the spring and watching women snip wool off the sheep and goats by hand as they gossiped and laughed. I remember the flashlights we relied on for light during inky-black winter nights and listening to the radio station KOMA from Oklahoma and when I heard Tina Turner belt out *River Deep Mountain High* for the first time. My father often complained about the short life of the batteries because his children wanted to listen to the radio. He used batteries for more important things, such as flashlights for checking on the flock, especially during lambing season.

I'm the paternal granddaughter of Edith, a tall, willowy Navajo woman. Her sharp and critical words were law. She had three daughters, Dora, Lutie, and Jeanette, and a son, Willie, my late father. My mother, Dorothy, is an in-law to my father's family. Edith had more than thirty grandchildren, including my sister, Earlene, my brothers Eisenhower and William, and me. My cousins are Rose, Delores, Hubert, Gary, David, Egbert, Albert, Clyde, Wilson, Robert, Doris, Nelson, Gilbert, Donald, Sam, Grace, Jimmy, Ben, Rena, Lula, Tyrone, and the late Jimmy and Faye.

The Navajo Nation is not so isolated from the rest of the world. The federal government demanded that Edith's grandchildren attend the Bureau of Indian Affairs boarding schools. Many of the grandsons went off the reservation for an education in the 1950s, 60s and well into the 70s, but some of Edith's granddaughters did not go to school because they had to tend the flocks of sheep. My cousin Clyde was drafted and served in the Vietnam War while my brother William received an education from Stanford University and currently teaches high school biology on the Nation.

When I retire, my hope is to return home to the Navajo Nation. But I feel I'm not yet ready for that transition, because I'm not jaded by the city life. I enjoy my career as a journalist. I'm also spoiled by modern accommodations, such as electricity and running water. I like life in the city because of the hot water that gushes out from the simple twist of a knob. I enjoy meals instantly warmed in the microwave oven, cooling air available at the press of a button, nearby grocery stores with varied supplies, paved roads, cyberspace, malls, movies, urban hiking, and a good neighborhood school for my daughter.

None of these accommodations exist where I grew up on the western part of the Navajo Nation. Development had been banned in the area west of Tuba City and east of the Colorado River since 1966 as a result of the Navajo-Hopi land dispute. I am also aware of the unemployment and the shortage of housing on the reservation. Services for Navajo senior citizens don't fulfill all elders' needs either.

Despite the lack of amenities my relatives did more than just survive. They thrived as shepherds roaming below shimmering blue skies and the barren desert. To my ancestors this was home, until their children received a modern education and—like me—enjoyed the American lifestyle. Maybe my retirement will just be spent planning the journey to my homeland.

Perhaps the most difficult part is my desire to roam like a Navajo child in the sweeping fields of sagebrush, or Tsa' Tah, near the Grand Canyon. I'd like to be that child on the Nation once more, but my mother and relatives scoff. They tell me the city has softened me or I no longer know the old ways or I speak funny Navajo. My mother also tells me I lack basic Navajo skills, such as slitting the throat of a sheep without making a bloody mess or addressing a Navajo elder in a proper manner or making a perfectly soft tortilla. She also informs me that my Navajo shepherding legs are history, and I'm no longer young.

In my mother's generation, Navajo women rely on the support of their relatives. When my mother, Dorothy, needs to run to the grocery store or needs someone to check on her livestock, my brother William responds. When she needs help reading her mail, my brother is there. When she needs water hauled or wood chopped to keep the home warm, her son William or her son-in-law Joe are there to help.

When she has a healing ceremony, relatives show up armed with the necessary goods for a successful event, including firewood, mutton, water, and blankets or fabric to pay a medicine man. When my mother needs her soiled laundry washed, my cousins Dee and Rose gladly oblige. They also give her a ride to the clinic for appointments. When my mother needs drinking water my brother William and cousin Gary haul gallons of water from the spigot to her home.

I doubt the government will provide adequate health care on the Nation when I hit sixty-five. Each administration changes Indian policies, and I assume it will ban free health care altogether for tribes and structure its service based on income soon. They chip away at the treaties. Though my daughters promise never to put me in a nursing home, they grew up with a different philosophy. The pull-yourself-up-by-your-bootstraps mentality is pounded into their lessons at school, and not much is taught about helping relatives. Perhaps this is what the government, my trustee, envisioned for me as a Navajo elder—getting off the federal dime and living off my savings just like any other American.

Maybe I'll turn into a Navajo snowbird, living on the Nation with my mother during the summer and in Phoenix during the winter. Maybe I'll volunteer my time and plan development for my homeland near the Grand Canyon and west of Tuba City. Maybe I'll continue to publish short stories about Navajo life. I have not thought of grandchildren, yet. But I'm sure they will be present in my life. I intend to teach them what it means to be a Navajo.

TWENTY NOTEWORTHY NAVAJO WOMEN

There are many Navajo women with remarkable accomplishments and contributions to Navajo life. Some have made their marks through medicine, law, education, and politics, while others have expressed their Navajo heritage and perseverance through art, architecture, entertainment, or even sports. Here is a small sample of extraordinary Navajo women.

Dr. Beulah Allen, the Navajos' first woman physician, continues to practice medicine on the Nation.

Dr. Lori Arviso Alvord, a graduate of Stanford University Medical School, was the first female Navajo surgeon to practice at the Gallup Indian Medical Center, in 1993. She is a surgeon, author, and professor.

Virginia Ballinger and **Arista La Russo** are two Navajo-inspired classic and contemporary fashion designers.

Claudeen Bates-Arthur (1942–2004), brilliant attorney who returned to the Navajo Nation after finishing law school at Arizona State University in 1974. Bates-Arthur was the first Navajo attorney general and the first female Navajo chief justice.

Ryneldi Becenti, from Fort Defiance, Arizona, was inducted into the Arizona State University Hall of Fame in 2005. She's the only American Indian to play for the Women's National Basketball Association and formerly played for the Phoenix Mercury.

D. Y. Begay, a Scottsdale resident originally from Chinle, is an award-winning rug weaver.

Sandra Begay Campbell, with Sandia National Laboratory, works tirelessly to improve nutrition for American Indian communities. Campbell received a bachelor of science degree in civil engineering from the University of New Mexico in 1987 and a master's degree in structural engineering from Stanford University in 1991. She also serves on the University of New Mexico Board of Regents.

Sharon Burch, a Navajo singer, blends the Navajo and English languages to write songs influenced by traditional Navajo prayers and chants. *Touch the Sweet Earth* received an INDIE award as Best Native American Album of 1995.

Alice Cling, an award-winning artist and businesswoman from Inscription House, molds her pottery to perfection.

Radmilla Cody, 1998 Miss Navajo Nation, is making a comeback as a female artist with a new CD, *Spirit of a Woman.*

Jennifer Nez Denetdale, Ph.D., a historian, lecturer, and professor at the University of New Mexico. Denetdale's book, *Reclaiming Dine History: The Legacies of Navajo Chief Manuelito and Juanita,* is scheduled for release in 2007.

Hope Lonetree-MacDonald, the daughter of controversial former leader Peter MacDonald, was the youngest woman to be elected to the Navajo Nation Council.

Lynda Lovejoy, from Crownpoint, New Mexico, was the first Navajo woman to make a presidential bid on the Navajo Nation. Although she lost the election, she changed history by edging out nine men to win the Navajo presidential primary. She is a former New Mexico lawmaker and served two four-year terms on the New Mexico Public Regulation Commission.

Ruth A. Roessel, a Round Rock elder, teaches Navajo philosophy to young students. She is an author and lecturer.

Marley Shebala, a *Navajo Times* reporter, has worked on the Nation for more than two decades. She writes about subjects from politics to environmental issues, creating awareness and debate over these topics.

Kimberly Silentman, an urban planner who joined a group of Navajo architects in 2005 to rearrange Window Rock, the capital of the tribe, which is set up in a hodge-podge fashion. She received her master's degree in urban and environmental planning from Arizona State University.

Catherine Smith, Pauline Whitesinger, and the late **Roberta Blackgoat** are elders who stood up to Congress and government officials when they tried to relocate Navajos off of land awarded to the neighboring Hopi tribe in the 1970s and 80s. The women brought the plight of Navajo residents to the attention of the world.

Luci Tapahonso, from Shiprock, New Mexico, is the author of *Sáanii Dahataal: The Women Are Singing* (1993), and *Blue Horses Rush In* (1999), which brought her international acclaim. Tapahonso obtained her bachelor and master's degrees from the University of New Mexico. She currently teaches at the University of Arizona.

Laura Tohe, author and poet, is a professor at Arizona State University. Her published books include *No Parole Today, Tseyi,* and *Sister Nations.*

Annie Dodge Wauneka (1918–1997), recipient of the Presidential Medal of Freedom in 1963 from President Lyndon B. Johnson, honoring her tireless crusade against tuberculosis. The daughter of the first modern Navajo chairman, Henry Dodge, also served on the Navajo Nation Council.

NAVAJO NATION FACTS AND FIGURES

These statistics present a few demographics of the Navajo people. The information is for 2005 and 2006 and is provided by the Comprehensive Economic Development Strategy of the Navajo Nation, the Navajo Nation Scholarship Office, and the Navajo Election Administration.

POPULATION

Total Navajo population: 298,215
Navajo Nation residents: 180,462
Female Navajo Nation residents: 51.8 percent
Male Navajo Nation residents: 48.2 percent
Navajo non-Nation resident distribution:
10,143 Phoenix, Arizona
7,889 Albuquerque, New Mexico
6,279 Gallup, New Mexico
5,793 Farmington, New Mexico
4,069 Flagstaff, Arizona
1,387 Tucson, Arizona
1,178 Salt Lake City, Utah
1,089 Los Angeles, California

ECONOMICS

Navajo Nation unemployment rate at a glance:
2004 – 48.04 percent
2003 – 47.57 percent
2002 – 46.07 percent
2001 – 42.16 percent
Navajo Nation poverty rate:
42.9 percent of Navajo individuals live below federal poverty level
40 percent of families live below federal poverty level on the Nation
53.1 percent of families with a female head of household live below federal poverty level

EDUCATION

Navajos graduating from high school:
75.5 percent of females, annually
69.3 percent of males, annually

COLLEGE EDUCATION AT A GLANCE FOR 2005-2006:

4,960 females enrolled in college
2,339 males enrolled in college
323 females earned bachelor degrees
102 males earned bachelor degrees
49 females earned master's degrees
17 males earned master's degrees
1 male earned a doctorate degree

TOP FIVE COLLEGE FIELDS OF STUDY PURSUED BY NAVAJO WOMEN:

Nursing
Elementary education
Liberal arts
Business administration
Early childhood education
Average age of a female Navajo college student: 27

FAMILY

Navajo Nation family census:
Navajo Nation average family size: 4.36 people
Navajo Nation median household income: $22,392
Average age of the Navajo Nation's population: 24
Navajo Nation single female heads of household: 24 percent

POLITICS

Navajo Nation registered voters: 98,294
Navajo women: 57,143
Navajo men: 41,151